# Marriage Essentials

## Focus on What Really Matters

Dr. Corey Allan

# Marriage Essentials

Focus on What Really Matters



For information about products and services contact:

Simple Marriage

www.simplemarriage.net

Dedicated to my wife, Pam, and my kids,
Sydney and Will

Thank you for being part of and joining
me on this great adventure in life.
You each bring richness to my life.
I love you.

# Contents

## PART ONE



## PART TWO

A foundational part of life is how you view relationships. As you delve into this book, answer these questions:

1. What is the purpose of relationships?
2. What is the purpose of marriage?
3. Why did I get married?

I'll answer the second question:

***Marriage is designed to refine us, to grow us up.***

Marriage provides a natural container designed for our growth. It creates a relationship above most other (if not all, which is where it should be) external relationships. Marriage is the only relationship that we freely choose, typically enter into with pomp and circumstance, and are encouraged to remain in for the rest of our lives.

This book is not about growing up, but it is important to keep this view in mind as you read through what follows.

This book is broken into two parts.

Part one covers the findings of a research study I conducted in 2009. I asked 1,028 people what they believe are the essential elements for a marriage or committed relationship to thrive. **Each chapter addresses one element; the**

**top ten, in rank order according to the research (from 1 to 10).**

Part two addresses five common issues married couples face in the course of marriage. Each of these issues often shift the focus away from the larger view of marriage, so they are covered in a way that help you focus on the essentials and not get bogged down with the unnecessary.

One last thing – I'm humbled and honored by the thousands of emails and comments I've received thus far from simplemarriage.net readers. Thank you for allowing me into your life and relationship.

What I receive from your reading what I write is far more than I give – thank you.

Strength and honor,

Corey

# PART ONE

# Communication

*The problem with communication . . . is the illusion that it has been accomplished. ~ George Bernard Shaw*

If there is one topic most people believe is important, it's this one: communication. Countless books on the market today attempt to address communication. You can earn a college degree in communication. So if communication is so important, and mastering this art would produce a better life, then why is it such a tough issue in marriage?

One reason may be because in marriage, everyone has already achieved the level of master communicator. This is especially true in conflictual relationships.

When looking at the subject of communication, you must begin with this fundamental truth:

**In marriage (as well as in any meaningful relationship), you cannot *not* communicate!**

Chances are when you and your spouse were having trouble communicating, the problem wasn't that you didn't hear each other; rather, you didn't like what your spouse had to say. Everything you do and don't do, say and don't

say, is a form of communication. So if my wife is trying to get my attention while I'm working on something else and I don't hear her—at that moment I'm communicating that what I'm doing is more important than her. Or if I set up the bedroom with candles, play soft music, and scatter rose petals around the bed, I've communicated something pretty clearly without saying a word. And if my wife comes into the room, steps over the rose petals, blows out the candles, climbs into bed, and goes to sleep—she has communicated something just as clearly.

There's no way around the issue of communication in marriage. So rather than taking you through some communication training or learning the proper use of "I" statements or even the difference between passive, assertive, and aggressive communication, let's look at how to better understand the messages we receive from our mate.

This is what communication in marriage is really all about.

## A brief history of communication

It is no surprise that men and women's minds are wired differently. Men are educated from birth to compete, judge, demand, and diagnose. We are very adept at seeing a problem that needs fixing and developing a way to fix it.

Unfortunately, this fix is according to the man, possibly not taking into account those around him. This is due in part to our learning to think and communicate in terms of what is "right" or what is "wrong."

To add to this, we often express our feelings in terms of what has been "done to us" rather than being independent of those around us. We mix up our needs and we ask for what we'd like using demands, guilt, or even the promise of rewards. This should come as no surprise since this is how many of us were raised by our parents.

At best, the basic way men think hinders communication and creates misunderstanding and frustration. At worst, it can lead to anger, depression, and even violence.

Women on the other hand have been exposed to conversations as a means for connection, sharing, and support. Early on, women interact with others more often for the intimate connection rather than a hierarchical status. Women are more likely to see people as interdependent and working in concert with one another.

Women tend to speak up first to address problems in marriage, as they are more relationally oriented. But speaking up may not be intended to fix the problems—it may be for closer connection. And keep in mind that while many relational problems may not be resolved (according to John Gottman, 63 percent of the issues faced in marriage are perpetual in nature), a deeper connection through them can be a tremendous opportunity for growth by both spouses.

**Learning how to understand the message in order to create a better relationship.**

To connect on a deeper level, we have to check ourselves throughout our conversations. Often when our emotions spike during a discussion, we will change the subject or attack the other person in order to help us feel better about whatever is going on at the moment.

My grandfather once said that when a person raises their voice, it's no longer about what is best for all involved and the current situation; it's about their power and pride.

The art of conversation at a deeper level:

1. Focus on the intention.

Marital conversations can often be simplified into one of two categories: a chance to become closer or a chance to create space. Humans vacillate between these two. If what you are really wanting is companionship, understanding, and compassion, then say so outright. If, on the other hand, you are wanting some space to chart your own course, speak up. Spending time together and apart are necessary components of every relationship.

2. Seek compassionate connection.

This is achieved primarily by a conversation not being tied to a particular outcome, like being right or talking the other person into doing something. Frequently when I experience what I consider to be misunderstandings, I am actually trying to get the other person to come around to my way of thinking. Focus on being clear with your side of the conversation and then clearly hearing the other side. This may mean you don't agree; so what. You are two separate individuals. You will not see eye to eye on everything.

**A conversation alternative**

By now you may be thinking it's time to try a new way to approach marital communication. At the same time, you may remember back to those times when, in spite of your best efforts, a conversation took a turn for the worse.

What happened?

Part of the answer might be found in the childhood expression, "Monkey see, monkey do." It turns out that our brains are hard-wired to mirror what we see.

You've read this before and it's worth repeating: In marriage (as well as in any meaningful relationship), you cannot *not* communicate.

In fact, some experts attribute up to 55 percent of communication as nonverbal body language. Examples of nonverbal body language are:

- Posture
- Facial expressions
- Appearance
- Voice
- Tone
- Expression in your eyes
- Smile, frown
- How you listen
- Your breathing
- Silence
- The way you move

So when you see the body language that naturally occurs in intense conversations—eye rolling, sighing, squirming, head shaking, looking down, looking away, glaring—your brain will naturally want to mirror what it sees. That's part of the biology that escalates communication from conversation to anger.

Depending on the intensity, face-to-face conversation can be threatening, intimidating, or even shut down communication.

It is hard to know your own thoughts if your partner grimaces while you are talking. There is a "lovelock"—a force field of verbal and nonverbal signals that say **agree, be nice,** or **get out.** Depending on your need for togetherness or separateness at the moment, you get sucked up into the "agree" or "be nice" signal or you push back with an "I'm out of here" signal.

We are seldom aware that we are sending out the lovelock signals.

One technique we can use to stay connected without getting sucked into the lovelock is to **walk and talk.**

Walking is a side-by-side activity that allows us to defuse the intense over focus on or hypersensitivity to body language. Walking interferes with the lovelock and our natural bent to mirror what we think we are getting, for good or bad. We can't see each other's face because we're looking ahead..

Walking dissipates the anxious energy that is part and parcel of talking about things that matter.

At the same time that anxious energy is being released, endorphins and serotonin—nature's feel-good chemicals—are being released in the brain, further enhancing your ability to tolerate anxiety.

The act of walking together while expressing differing and/or conflicting thoughts, ideas, and positions is a physical representation of differentiation—emotional maturity.

*I can hold on to my own ideas about something that is important to me while walking by your side, caring for you, heading in the same direction (together through life), with the same outcome (headed for home at the end of the walk).*

Face-to-face communication comes with pressure for one or both parties to cave in to a "we-ness" mind-set. Face to face can become more of an endpoint—where we end up when there are two whole people in a relationship. You can gauge how well you are doing in the relationship by how comfortable you are with a face-to-face conversation about an intense topic.

If you can't take a walk together because of a physical impairment, young kids (use a stroller), or bad weather (there's no such thing as bad weather, only bad gear), shift to side-by–side conversation. Sit next to each other on the couch, **but do not face each other:** just stay engaged. This will alleviate some of the intensity and enable you to focus on your part of the discussion as well as listening to your partner.

Try it this week. Walk and talk together for a minimum of thirty minutes a day and see what difference it makes.

# Trust

trust: (noun) firm belief in the reliability, truth, ability, or strength of someone or something (Webster's Dictionary)

In most every poll or research study conducted on relationships, a key component required for the relationship to thrive is trust. I hear it all the time from couples I work with.

*"I need to be able to trust him."*

*"I trusted her."*

These phrases are commonplace in marriage.

My question: "Trust your spouse to do *what* exactly?" It seems that trust is often used as a tool rather than a foundational belief. Let's look at how this commonly plays out.

"I'll tell you about me, but only if you tell me about you."

"If you don't, I won't either. But I want to, so you have to."

"I'll go first, and then you have to tell me too: it's only fair."

"If I go first, you have to make me feel secure, because I need to be able to ***trust*** you."

Sound familiar? Shouldn't we have trust in relationships? Yes—trust is vital, —but there's a limit to the role it should play.

Trust is frequently thrown around in marriage as an attempt to control situations and make things "safe" for oneself. We think we must be able to trust our partner, thus freeing us to be ourselves.

When I say I trust my partner, I'm actually saying I'm willing to reveal more of myself to them.

So is that really about them or me?

I may be splitting hairs here, but it's an important topic to explore.

Throughout the course of therapy, inevitably couples who've experienced some sort of betrayal or affair will bring up the broken level of trust in the relationship. But isn't this statement, "We have to work on rebuilding the trust in the marriage," really another way of the hurt spouse saying, "I want you to make this up to me"?

Trust is really more about oneself than it is the other person. Trust is found in the integrity of oneself (and others).

Trust is typically reciprocity based; meaning, if I give it, it must be reciprocated. Again, this is setting up a power struggle and an attempt to control something you cannot possibly control—namely, your spouse.

At lower levels of growing up in relationship, trust is better termed *dependency*.

So here's the rub: How much dependency can you place on another fallible human being? A being who is likely more concerned about themselves than you (their concern is valid as this helps perpetuate the species; the concern for self is also what creates the possibility for choice, and ultimately love, in relationships).

If you no longer have trust in another person as a key, you begin the process of self-definition where you literally start squaring off with your partner and defining *yourself*, but not simply in relationship to each other.

You begin to see that the real issue is what you have been doing to yourself. Your stance might become, "The real issue is what I have been doing to me. You take care of you. My issue is me."

In a couple who lacks emotional maturity, the agreements about what will go on in the relationship often are contingent on the meaning of trust. This may mean that one partner will give up something (i.e., drugs, alcohol, commitment to work, porn, even extramarital affairs) in order to deprive their partner of the same thing.

For example, one person wants to be in a monogamous relationship, so they give up extramarital sex in order to deprive their partner of sex with other people. It's a classic exchange-based agreement. The only problem is that five years from now, when you (either partner) are ticked off, you turn to your partner and say: "You owe me; it's your fault I haven't screwed anybody else. I gave it up for you." The partner has become emotionally fused.

At higher levels of emotional maturity, these agreements go like this: "I want to be in a monogamous relationship, so I'm not having an affair. You don't owe me for it, because I'm not doing it for you, I'm doing it for me. Now if you have an affair, the only thing I ask is that you tell me."

Monogamy, or more appropriately everything in the marriage, is no longer based on exchange and reciprocity (i.e. trust). It results from a unilateral commitment to oneself. You no longer feel controlled by your spouse. You relinquish your spouse as an extension of yourself and your own gratification. And what happens, oddly enough, is that you end up having all the trust that you need. And when trust is inevitably broken in some form or fashion, you also know you can handle whatever happens.

# Love

Love—something people throughout the centuries have sought, fought for, died for, dreamed of, longed for, ached over, and hopefully tasted. But love has also been largely misunderstood. Most people seem to believe love is a feeling. While this is true, it's not the entire story.

Love is a process. Love will produce action.

And action is love's litmus test.

Love is not an answer to things insomuch as it is a force behind the answer.

And the problem you may have experienced with love is the confusion often associated with the "love" you felt at the beginning of a relationship. Remember the feelings of euphoria and the longing to simply spend time with your partner when you first met? What you were experiencing back then actually wasn't love. Sorry to burst your bubble, but what you were under was a chemically induced spell.

Look at it this way.

You meet your soon-to-be love interest and are attracted to something about them. Personality, looks, character, sense of humor—you name it, something caused them to stand out. You muster up the courage to initiate a conversation (or you respond to their gesture), and you head down the road you think is paved with love.

Actually, it is the nature of all dating and pre-married people to be idealistically distorted. It is wish fulfillment; you see what you wish to see in order to protect the feelings you believe your partner has caused.

During the initial stages of an intimate relationship, your brain produces a chemical called Phenylethylamine, a naturally occurring chemical found in your brain as well as in other substances, like chocolate. Phenylethylamine, also known as the "love drug," produces feelings of euphoria and alertness, and improves your sense of well-being. In the beginning stages of a love relationship, your brain is flooded with this chemical.

Phenylethylamine is produced in the emotional center of your brain called the amygdala, and this flooding will last from six months to two years, which is about the same amount of time it takes many couples to meet, fall in love, get engaged, and get married. So after you return from your honeymoon, or shortly thereafter, the "love drug" has begun wearing off and you're now faced with being married to a person you may be seeing without the rose-colored glasses for the first time. This is also why there are many people who've woken up one morning a couple of years into the marriage and said to themselves, "Who is this person I'm married to? Where'd the person I was dating and engaged to go?"

We long for the feelings we experienced when we were dating. Perhaps you've been there as well. You want to flood your brain with another dose of the "love drug." The problem is, you can't go backward in life or in relationships. Instead, you must go forward. You must realize that your chemically altered relationship is a thing of the past and work on growing into your relationship of the present and future. Phenylethylamine has run its course and now you can work on increasing your level of the "bonding" chemical known as Oxytocin.

Oxytocin runs deep in the brain. It isn't a chemical that floods and fades; it's produced and hangs around a while. Oxytocin is created during deep and profound moments with another person, most notably crisis (and tragedy) and sex (specifically orgasm). It is the experience of going through both the great and the tough times in life that bond us most.

Based on this, I'm not going to recommend that you put yourself and your marriage through rough times intentionally, although feel free to have as many orgasms as you can together (doctor's orders ☺).

But you can learn to love more.

In his book *The Art of Loving*, Erich Fromm's key point is that love is indeed an art. And any art requires knowledge, effort, and a good deal of practice. You cannot expect to pick up a musical instrument and immediately play a perfect piece. A master sculptor's greatest work is not in their first attempt. Yet most people do not believe (or at least do not act as if) they have anything to learn about love.

Fromm explains several faulty premises of society's belief about love.

1. Love is about being loved rather than loving.

2. Love's greatest step is finding an object to love rather than developing an ability to love.

3. Love is a consumer transaction: people behave as if love is about obtaining as good a "package" in the other person as they are prepared to "pay for" by exchange. It's the classic exchange-based relationship, much like a mobile

phone contract: I will give you safety, security, companionship, etc., and you will give me sex, support, encouragement, etc.

4. Love is about "falling" in love, rather than the permanent state of being in love or staying in love or standing in love. In this situation, as intimacy grows and mystery shrinks, disappointment and boredom will kill off the initial excitement.

As a believer in God and the stories in the Bible, I've often wondered what the purpose of the tree in the Garden of Eden was. God tells Adam that he is free to eat of any tree in the garden except one. Why? This is an idea I struggled with for quite a while.

Why, if God knows our propensity to do our own thing and follow our own path, would He allow a way out—knowing we would most likely take it?

The answer is simple. **If there wasn't a way out of the relationship, there couldn't be love.**

At the very core of love is the freedom to choose.

Love lets you go.

Love lets you be you.

God had to provide a way out of the relationship for there to be a relationship. Marriage is the same. I realize we don't like to admit this, but marriage is fragile. Divorce is an option. Your partner could choose to move on to someone else.

He could choose to spend more time at work than at home with you. She could choose to live through the kids and their activities rather than with you.

Your partner could choose countless other things than you.

There is no way you can control your partner and force them to love you. A marriage in which one partner seeks to control and change the other partner is simply manipulation; it has nothing to do with love.

# Respect

R-E-S-P-E-C-T

Respect is a basic foundation for civilized society; perhaps for uncivilized societies as well.

In every group of people there are written and unwritten rules the group is expected to follow. And all of these rules are based on the premise of respect.

Respect for others. Respect for life. Respect for yourself.

When there is respect for others and self, communities are more secure and stable. If everyone respected their neighbors, there would be no crime. And it's easy to spot the families where respect for each other is lacking or non-existent.

But what about when you narrow it down to marriage?

If respect is essential for a marriage to thrive, then the fate of your marriage is in your hands. It boils down to this:

**Respect begets respect.**

For most of us, it's easy to recognize respect when it comes our way. But it's even easier to spot the *lack* of respect. So rather than discussing what respect is, let's briefly look at what it isn't.

Dr. John Gottman is one of the most renowned marriage researchers to date. Through his research of married couples he can predict the end of a marriage relationship with a stunning 93 percent accuracy. Dr. Gottman has identified some communication styles he calls the Four Horsemen of the Apocalypse. (If you're not familiar with biblical references, the Four Horsemen represent a metaphor for conquest, war, hunger, and death associated with the end times.)

When respect is lacking in a marriage, it can be difficult to know where to begin. Just like trust, respect begins and ends with you. If you want to know how to instill respect back into your marriage, start by eliminating the four horsemen.

The four horsemen are **criticism**, **contempt**, **defensiveness**, and **stonewalling**, and contempt is the most lethal of the four. Contempt is the acid rain on a marriage, withering affection and destroying hope. It is also completely devoid of respect. For a marriage to have respect (among other good qualities) you simply have to get rid of the four horsemen—and contempt is the most destructive. In fact, it is so harmful that you must have contempt for contempt in your relationship.

**The first destructive horseman in a relationship is criticism.** Understanding the difference between criticizing and complaining is more than semantics, because criticism is the slippery slope that slides into contempt.

Criticisms creep in when complaints are ignored. Criticisms are global attacks on character and self-worth, and target the shortcomings of the other. Complaints are objective statements of unmet needs.

An effective complaint is one that:

1. Starts softly, with a request for help ("I need your help.")

   Observes an action or behavior ("When there are stacks of mail on the kitchen table and counters, . . ")

2. States the impact of that action or behavior (". . . I react badly to the clutter.")

Defines the desired change in behavior ("I'd like to keep the kitchen table and counters clear.")

3. Asks for input on how to achieve the outcome ("What are you willing to do to help have a less cluttered kitchen and a calmer me?")

**The second horseman is contempt.** Contempt is intentionally abusing your spouse verbally, emotionally, and/or psychologically.

Contempt expresses the complete absence of any admiration or respect and is delivered with insults, name-calling, hostile humor, mockery, and body language.

Contempt is toxic and its presence is an indication of a disintegrating marriage. It must be eliminated.

If criticism and contempt are a regular part of your relational style, think about counseling to help you take a different shape. These two horsemen grew up in childhood wounds such as parental criticism, shaming, belittling, or excessive demands, so they can be tough to shake as adults.

**The third horseman is defensiveness.** Defensiveness is a natural reaction to being criticized or treated contemptuously. It's also a way of sidestepping responsibility. If you are ignoring complaints and failing to contribute creative solutions, those complaints are likely to become criticisms you naturally want to defend against. Remember this mantra:

***Don't attack. Don't defend. Don't withdraw.***

Marriage is for better or worse. Stay present, especially when the going gets rough.

**The fourth horseman is stonewalling.** When you stonewall, you avoid the hard work of growing up, either because you're unaware of your own feelings or you are afraid of conflict. Rather than dealing directly with the issue or with your partner, you check out by tuning out, turning away, engaging in busyness or obsessive behaviors. You simply stop relating to the most important people in your life.

Gottman's research clearly demonstrates that conflict is not the cause of unhappy marriages: happy and unhappy couples fight about the same things.

**It's how conflict is handled that makes the difference between a disaster or master marriage.**

Most couples wait for six years—six years!—after they know their relationship is in serious trouble before they seek counseling. Evidence continues to mount that both individual and family therapy save money by cutting health expenditures, reducing employee absenteeism, and boosting productivity.

Start where you are in your relationship. Use the tools you have—blogs, books, therapists, coaches. Do what you can to take responsibility for your part by becoming the best *you* you can be.

To repeat: Start where you are. Use what you have. Do what you can.

Remember what I stated at the beginning of this chapter:

**Respect begets respect.**

Think of it this way. Relationships are embedded in nature—once you know there are four seasons in every year and it's cold in winter and hot in summer, it's easier to change your clothes than it is to change the seasons. In fact, it's not possible to change the seasons—and it's also not possible to change your spouse, or anyone else.

It's only possible to change yourself.

The only way to instill more respect in your marriage is to treat your spouse with more respect. In doing so, you also treat yourself with more respect.

Here's a new version of the Serenity Prayer, designed to reflect these thoughts. Instead of Serenity Prayer, I call it the Power of One.

GOD GRANT ME
THE SERENITY TO ACCEPT THE PEOPLE I CANNOT CHANGE
THE COURAGE TO CHANGE THE ONE I CAN
AND THE WISDOM TO KNOW—
THAT ONE IS ME.

# Commitment

Marriage is work.

Marriage is struggle.

Then again, any close relationship is. And for that matter, so is anything of value in life.

I have been asked, "What makes a marriage last?" "What's the secret to a lasting marriage?"

The answer is actually simple (*simple is not to be confused with easy*).

Before I divulge the secret, let's tackle a few marriage myths.

Thanks to popular press and Hollywood, what actually takes place in marriage is poorly displayed. People tend to think that marriage will be a lifelong romantic escapade along the shore at sunset before returning home for the nightly passionate adventure enveloped in silk sheets with their lover. I know you've bought into this idea somewhat.

To prove my point, see if you can easily complete this phrase: "and they all lived . . ."

The honeymoon is over, morning breath has set in, your partner sees you for who you are, and you see your partner for who they are. You realize that marriage requires more of you. The dream of marriage has been replaced with the reality of marriage. You and your spouse don't see eye to eye on everything. You've slept on the couch at least once in your married life. You've ridden a roller coaster of feelings—closeness, distance, passion, boredom, joy, sadness.

When you get right down to it, **marriage is not about happiness. Marriage is about two people growing up and becoming better humans.**

Nowhere else are we faced with the task of growth more than marriage.

So what's the secret to making marriage last?

**Two people who choose to stay married.** That's it.

It's a commitment.

Marriage is choice. Choice of partner, choice of self, choice of growth, even choice of passion and adventure.

If this seems simplistic, it is.

Commitment gets a bad rap.

Sure, it involves sacrifice and effort, but it's worth it for something you believe in. Something you want in life.

Every athlete who excels in their sport has commitment. Elite athletes recognize that a great deal of time, labor, and physical pain are required to accomplish the necessary level of training if they are to perform at an optimal level. Lance Armstrong, seven-time winner of the Tour de France, has said he doesn't think he would enjoy life as much if it didn't involve a certain amount of physical suffering in training. Sacrifice, in addition to being necessary to accomplishment, is equated with the goal. So is commitment.

Carrying out the actions of commitment represents the value of marriage, and becomes satisfying in itself.

When you look at your marriage as a process for growth and experiencing more in life, it makes commitment to the marriage easier.

Focusing on the desire for your partner to change or do things differently means focusing on something you can't control. But when you decide to grow, do something different, change the things you don't like about yourself, you take charge of your own life as well as your relationship.

How you view what happens in life and love will determine the outcome. When you have a disagreement, could it actually be a time to grow closer? Or a time to better understand your spouse? When you sense your spouse is pulling away, maybe it's an opportunity to more fully engage. To grow into a new level of commitment in your life.

There are several aspects of commitment.

First, the positive aspect is what you do to nurture your relationship with your spouse. Planning an evening out, cooking a meal together, or taking time to talk each day.

Second, the negative aspect is what you avoid doing to prevent distance from developing in the relationship and outside forces from dividing you, for example, not making yourself available for close relationships with the opposite sex, not spending the entire weekend at the golf course, not taking the job that requires being away from home three weeks out of the month.

And third is the aspect of commitment that Scott Stanley refers to in his book *The Heart of Commitment* as "met-commitment."—the commitment to being committed. Stated another way, this is a belief in doing what you say you will do.

So does being committed to marriage mean you do so at all costs?

Absolutely not!

Everyone has deal breakers when entering a marriage; things they will not tolerate in a relationship. A typical one would be a spouse having sex with someone else. Acts such as this call into question commitment not only to your marriage, but more importantly commitment to yourself.

Will you stick to your beliefs and values? Will you follow through with actions based on your beliefs and values?

**Commitment only goes as far as the action associated with it.**

**Many people have the intention of staying committed to their marriage and spouse, and many also realize that this implies translating commitment into actions, yet they fail to do it.**

At the same time, many people have a commitment to themselves, yet they fail to follow through.

**Commitment to yourself is where it all begins.**

You must develop an honesty within yourself that counters the elasticity of thinking and self-deception that your mind is capable of.

Humans have a tendency to develop a private logic, or set of beliefs, that are comfortable.

You may avoid seeking the real truth, which can be uncomfortable. For example, it feels better if you can believe that the larger share of the blame for a problem lies outside yourself. Or you may want to believe you can enjoy the independence of single life within the unity of married life. Or you may want the satisfaction of being right and in control, as well as the deep connection with your spouse that is possible only when you give up these things.

I think if marriage is to be lasting and satisfying, you must periodically evaluate the nature of your commitment, namely, you must examine your actions and behavior patterns, and then determine what those actions and behaviors are saying about your commitment.

**Commitment is demonstrated in action as well as belief and choice.**

# Honesty

*No man has a good enough memory to make a successful liar.* - Abraham Lincoln

If asked, you probably will say you're an honest person. Meaning, you don't blatantly lie.

But what if I asked if you occasionally omit some things; how would you answer?

It's part of our creation and design to be honest. We all seem to have an innate sense that honesty is the best policy, that lying hurts others as well as ourselves.

At the same time, however, have we reached a point where we feel it's okay to omit certain details while still feeling as though we're being honest?

The world in which we live is filled with lies.

I'll admit, I have a lying problem. Mine aren't the big lies, the things like "No, I don't remember sending that memo, Senator" or "I did not have sexual relations with that woman." No, mine are the little lies. The half-truths. "Yes, let's definitely get together for coffee soon." "We can't buy a toy now, son, the toy store is closed."

The problem with lying—it creates an alternate reality. And trying to keep up with multiple realities is anything but simple and easy.

One of the first things I counsel couples who come to see me is to up their honesty level. Not that they're lying to each other all the time, or even occasionally, but when you up the honesty level in life, while things may get worse temporarily, eventually they will get better.

You can begin by upping the honesty level with yourself.

**Many bad things in our lives originate from not being honest with ourselves and others.**

Unfortunately, we all have the ability to rationalize and justify our thoughts and actions. In fact, many people can get good enough at it to actually believe their rationalization is the truth. But when it comes to honesty, your gut knows the truth.

Dishonesty keeps you awake at night, or wakes you up in the middle of the night. It gives you the twinge of anxiety in your stomach. And it comes out in your body language and facial expressions.

Honesty, on the other hand, allows you to rest peacefully. To act according to your values and integrity. And to develop deeper, more meaningful relationships.

**Honesty leads to simplicity.**

Life carries with it a great deal of energy when you're honest with yourself and others. You gain others' trust easily because you live according to your word. You reach a point where you can let your yes be yes and your no be no. And, as the honesty between you and others increases, so does the synergy.

Honesty in life and marriage is not just the best policy; it's the only policy. A simple marriage is unattainable without it.

**Do these pants make me look fat?**

And since you probably are wondering if you should be honest when your wife asks you, "Do these pants make look fat?" look her in the eye and with a playful smile reply, "I don't know, I'd have to see you without the pants on."

# Laughter

*The art of medicine consists of amusing the patient while nature cures the disease.* ~ Voltaire

*We cannot really love anybody with whom we never laugh.* ~ Agnes Repplier

Have you and your spouse ever found something to be funny and you reach a point where you feed off each other? Most often this happens when you're watching a somber play, or in the middle of church, or even during dinner at a quiet restaurant. But your giggles feed the other's and off you go.

Laughter is contagious. It's also beneficial to life and marriage.

**Benefits of Laughter**

- Reduction of stress and tension
- Stimulation of the immune system
- An increase of natural painkillers in the blood
- A decrease in systemic inflammation
- Reduction of blood pressure

- Lifts your spirits
- Brings couples closer together
- Can help keep a relationship fresh.

There are other medical benefits than the ones listed above. Our cardiovascular and respiratory systems, for example, benefit more from twenty seconds of robust laughter than from three minutes of exercise on a rowing machine. Through laughter, muscles release tension and neurochemicals are released into the bloodstream, creating the same feelings the long-distance joggers experience as "runner's high."

It has also been discovered that for some hospital patients, ten minutes of genuine belly laughter would have an anesthetic effect that could give a couple hours of pain-free sleep.

Humor brings more than just physiological benefits to a husband and wife. Humor helps us cope.

Humor relieves the tension that can build up between people. It also will bond you with those you laugh with. Research has found that laughter produces Oxytocin, a chemical in the brain also referred to as the bonding chemical.

Learning to laugh a little more just may save your life, not to mention your marriage. To paraphrase Henry Ward Beecher, "A marriage without a sense of humor is like a wagon without springs—jolted by every pebble in the road."

Still not convinced? Take it from these professionals: Legendary comedian Bob Hope said laughter is an "instant vacation." Jay Leno says, "You can't stay mad at somebody who makes you laugh." And Bill Cosby says, "If you can find humor in anything, you can survive it."

Studies reveal that individuals who have a strong sense of humor are less likely to experience burnout and depression and they are more likely to enjoy life in general—including their marriage.

So lighten up. Stop taking yourself so seriously. And while we're on the subject, stop taking life so seriously; we aren't getting out of it alive anyway!

# Sex

- ★ Have sex.
- ★ Often.
- ★ Slow down.
- ★ Connect.
- ★ Slow down.
- ★ Talk.
- ★ Slow down.
- ★ Enjoy each other.
- ★ Be 100 percent present.
- ★ Take your time.
- ★ Slow down.
- ★ Talk.
- ★ Listen.
- ★ Use words when necessary.
- ★ Focus on quality, not quantity.

I could end this chapter here; the above says it all. But figuring this will likely be one of the more popular chapters, I want to dive into a deeper aspect of sex between two people: the fine art of doing and being done.

Do you know what it feels like to have your spouse *do* you—not just bringing you to orgasm or having intercourse—but really *do* you?

Do you know what it feels like to *do* your spouse?

At its core is power. And the fact is, negotiating power is part of every human relationship.

Almost everything in our society teaches equality, including many therapists. The message they try to get across is this: the ideal partner is to be one of absolute equality in every area of the relationship.

I've got news for you – equality has no place when it comes to eroticism. The ability to take your partner (or be taken by them) embodies a lusty, lascivious eagerness for pleasure. This isn't crudeness—quite the opposite—it's a deliberate intent to arouse (and satisfy) passion.

If you're one of many who've yet to experience this level of passion and eroticism in marriage, or if you've had a taste of it but it faded over time, don't worry. For most people, the eroticism and level of passion I'm talking about ripens in later life.

It involves tapping into the male and female energy found in a couple's union. The *Yin and Yang,* to use Eastern terms. When you and your partner tap into, you form the energy loop that Tantric sex (an ancient Eastern spiritual practice) has focused on for centuries.

This energy creates the "follow the connection" types of sexual encounters—those times when your spouse "knows" you completely and can send you over the edge whenever *they* choose to do so. **In essence, they have power over you—and wielding this power produces an erotic pleasure within themselves.**

Many people in our culture are afraid of this power. It's labeled as bad or something dirty. It's something "nice people" would *never* do. But, it's an aspect of every one of us.

So how do you reach this level of eroticism and sexual passion?

The short answer is, grow up and develop this part of you.

For many, this part of themselves is yet to be born. If you think it has reached maturity in you, answer this: When your partner really ticks you off, how do you react? Can you lovingly and passionately *integrate* the anger and aggression you feel toward your spouse and turn it into something useful and life-giving? Or are you more likely to react to the anger and do anything you can to get away from your spouse? Can the fact that your spouse is different and separate from you be a *turn-on* rather than a turn-off?

Fully creating this energy involves learning how to acknowledge the aggression and anger toward your spouse (which is in all of us), soothing yourself, mastering yourself, and "growing" through the discomfort.

When we climb into bed with our spouse, we each carry different expectations, hopes, plans, and passions to the experience about to unfold.

Let's face it, on a basic biological level, men and women are different. Arousal, pleasure, eroticism, power, even orgasms are different.

Men can be quite envious of a woman's orgasm. Look at the differences between us: When a man has an orgasm, while the feeling is great, it seems to pale in comparison to a woman's. A woman is capable of full-body orgasms, seeming to pulsate like waves throughout her entire body. Plus—and the biggest source of male envy—a woman is capable of wave after wave. A man has to have some recovery time. Just look at the facial expressions of the two sexes and you'll get confirmation of the difference.

So rather than focus on the differences that separate you and your spouse, what if you each brought more of yourself to the party? Could you handle that?

Many of you will quickly reply . . . yes!

Really, though?

Think about it this way: If you are a male, can you really handle a full-grown woman? One who knows what she wants sexually and how she wants it? A woman in touch with her raw, animalistic nature? This will require more of you, perhaps *much* more of you! It may mean that after you've experienced your orgasm, you have to stay around for hers. It may mean you have to submit to her power, or you have to overpower her and truly *take* her.

And if you are a female, are you ready for a full-grown man? Someone in touch with his power, or what Robert Bly refers to as the "deep male"? A man in tune with his raw, animalistic nature? This, too, will require more of you.

If you're interested in creating this part of you and your relationship, here are a few ideas to help you get started. Realize, however, that this developing takes time and growth to be fully born out in your life and marriage. And also realize that this type of eroticism and passion can only develop in the space between you. It requires two individuals who bring their entire selves to the marriage—their power, fear, mistakes, and vulnerabilities.

**Slow down.** This is the number one thing I tell every couple I work with when it comes to sex. I understand the desire to rush things, because the longer the process of sex lasts, the more likely things within you will surface that make you uncomfortable. Slow down. When the discomfort arises, face it head on.

**Breathe.** Much like the previous point, spend time just breathing. Focus on your breathing, and match your spouse's breathing.

**Speak up, but not with words.** Use your body. Your movements. Your power. Watch each other feel the process. And let yourself be seen. Use words when needed for direction, but also use moans, groans . . . you get the idea.

Surrendering and growing into this part of you is no simple matter.

*Doing* your spouse, or allowing yourself to be *done,* involves "standing on your own two feet." It's not forcing yourself on your spouse—it's a letting go with your spouse.

Tapping into eroticism and new levels of passion requires tremendous personal integrity. It takes a great deal of integrity to face head-on the demands and challenges of exploring your sexual potential.

But you know what? Every one of us has untapped sexual potential just waiting to be discovered.

If you place two violins next to each other and pluck a string on one, the corresponding string on the other will vibrate. It recognizes its own wave.

Marital sex can be the same. You and your spouse can resonate with each other, creating your own music together.

Now close this book and go find your spouse. Only this time, don't just make music together, create a symphony!

# Friendship

"He's like my best friend."

"She's the best friend in my life."

These are common statements and beliefs about a relationship with our spouse. That they must be our friend, no, best friend—as well as all the other roles a spouse plays in marriage.

While I don't discount that there should be friendship between husband and wife, having him or her as your best friend will be the death-nail to the marriage. To clarify, I'm referring to best friend here as a primary and/or sole outlet of your relational needs.

When you first met your spouse, *ideally* you were both living lives that were fulfilling and interesting (note the emphasis on "ideally"—if you and/or your spouse didn't have a lot going on when you first met, the relationship was already in really big trouble). One reason your spouse was attractive was the life they were living apart from you. The lives you were living before you met were an important part of what made each of you who you were.

As you began spending more time together and getting to know one another, you likely had less time to engage in the things you were doing before you met. Some couples go so far as to completely give up everything they previously found fulfilling and important in order to spend time together. The problem with this is, as you became fused, you became more and more dependent on each other to meet your individual needs.

That's the problem with your spouse being your best friend.

As you give up those things you find fulfilling and important for the sake of the relationship, this places a tremendous burden on your spouse to fill the void of whatever you gave up. And this burden will create neediness and dependency, as well as resentment and boredom.

**One of the best things you can do for your spouse is have a couple of great same-sex friendships.**

Every marriage needs space between the spouses. It is within this space that you find energy, passion, eroticism, quiet time, and personal fulfillment.

While I believe that friendship within the marriage is vital for the relationship, close friendships outside of the marriage are equally important, especially if you want a marriage with lots of passion, eroticism, adventure, and energy. **One of the biggest killers of passion in marriage is all the meaningless time spouses spend together. And this monotonous coexistence is what often comes to define most marriages.**

If you want to create a great marriage full of energy, adventure, passion, and love, spend some time away from your spouse with your friends.

**"Marriage" taken from "The Prophet" Khalil Gibran**

*But let there be spaces in your togetherness,*
*And let the winds of the heavens dance between you.*
*Love one another but make not a bond of love:*
*Let it rather be a moving sea between the shores of your souls.*
*Fill each other's cup but drink not from one cup.*
*Give one another of your bread but eat not from the same loaf.*
*Sing and dance together and be joyous, but let each one of you be alone,*
*Even as the strings of a lute are alone though they quiver with the same music.*
*Give your hearts, but not into each other's keeping.*
*For only the hand of Life can contain your hearts.*

*And stand together, yet not too near together:*

*For the pillars of the temple stand apart,*

*And the oak tree and the cypress grow not in each other's shadow.*

# Compatibility

"We simply weren't compatible." "We must have been made for each other, we fit together so well." A common belief is that somewhere out there in the universe is a *soul mate* for each of us. Someone we were made for. Someone who just clicks with our makeup and design.

While there is something to personality types and the idea that some "types" go better with other "types," I don't think there is a soul mate for each of us. Or, more aptly put, if there is, there are several hundreds of them.

It is more appropriate to look at system compatibility than personal.

When you met and married your spouse, your systems collided. And ever since, the two systems have been sorting out how to create a new system. A new way of doing things. Your parents did this. Your kids will as well.

By applying the lens of growing up to marriage, you can see compatibility in an entirely different way.

At a foundational level, you and your spouse are only together because of a similar level of "growth" in your life thus far. As you grew up in your family, you developed to a certain emotional maturity level. Put in psychobabble, you reached a level of differentiation. And theory states that you will meet and fall in love with someone at the same level of differentiation as yourself. Otherwise, the way they do life and handle conflict, stress, heartache, and frustration would be so foreign that you would not understand it or tolerate it.

This is why our spouse so often has traits similar to one or both of our parents. It's what we know and understand.

So to answer the question of whether you and your spouse are compatible . . . Yes. Otherwise you wouldn't have gotten together in the first place. But what do you do when you feel so incompatible at times?

You should already know the answer to this one . . .grow up!

You reached a level of growth in your family of origin. This growth is often at or just below your parents' level of growth. You then meet and fall in love with someone at the same level and you begin the process of spurring one another along to new and higher levels of growth.

Relationships, specifically marital relationships, create natural containers designed for our growth. And the growth between the spouses will be at the same level, or, at the most, one will be a half step ahead of the other. So when you or your spouse are a half step ahead, it places tremendous pressure on the system. Again, apply the previous idea to this point. If you grow beyond your spouse, or if your differentiation level far exceeds your spouse's, either the system will get things back to the previous level, the other spouse will grow up to meet the other's level, or the relationship will fall apart.

This pressure happens all the time in marriage. It's natural.

Let's say your spouse wants to begin a workout routine. At first, you're all for it. But after a while, you don't like the amount of time your spouse spends away from you. While you like the way they look from working out and the newfound confidence they exude, you don't like the additional looks they are getting from others. You want things to go back to the way they were. You are now faced with the natural process of growth playing out in your marriage.

If your spouse continues on their current level of differentiation, you are forced to either:

1. dominate your spouse,

2. submit to your spouse,

3. withdraw physically or emotionally from the relationship, or

4. grow up.

**Marriage can hold your spouse's happiness hostage—and the ransom price is your personal growth.**

The reason for this is your compatibility, as well as your incompatibility.

Each of us faces the choices of stifling our spouse's growth, destroying our spouse's happiness, or growing ourselves up.

These forced-choice systemic dilemmas are referred to by Dr. David Schnarch as "crucibles"—severe tests of selfhood and personal integrity built into every emotionally committed relationship.

Rather than blaming incompatibility for the stress and troubles in your marriage, you will be better served if you use the natural process of growing up in marriage in order to experience all this life (and marriage) has to offer.

# PART TWO

# Simple Contentment

*The secret of happiness, you see, is not found in seeking more, but in developing the capacity to enjoy less. ~ Socrates*

Many things get in the way of our relationships. Perhaps the biggest issue is discontentment. The Dalai Lama once said, "*When you are discontent, you always want more, more, more. Your desire can never be satisfied. But when you practice contentment, you can say to yourself, 'Oh yes, I already have everything that I really need.'*"

A dominant question for us, sadly, isn't what's my purpose or why am I here, it's what's wrong and how do we fix it. This question shapes our worldview, our parenting, and our relationships.

We live in a fix-it society, as if everything wrong in the world can be "fixed." This idea is largely responsible for the consumerism in society. If you believe there is something wrong or missing in your life, then some company or industry has a product that will correct what's wrong, or at least make you feel better about it.

Watch any amount of TV and you'll be bombarded with this idea. I've even fallen victim to this in my own life. I'll be surfing the web and come across the latest techno gadget, and for a while, I'm consumed with the desire to get it. It's as if the gadget will fix something missing or lacking in my life.

Keep this truth in mind: Focusing solely on what's wrong is a black hole.

When it comes to marriage, this type of thinking is common. How often do you hear or say, "When are you going to . . . ?" or "You always . . ." Arguments in marriage are caused by focusing on what's wrong.

It's important to realize that in committed relationships, roughly two-thirds of the problems are not resolvable. Two-thirds!

With the amount of issues in marriage that aren't resolvable, how do you create a lasting and passionate marriage?

It begins with practicing contentment in life.

What you focus on . . . grows.

This philosophy is true. If you focus solely on what's wrong, everything will appear wrong. Don't believe me?

Watch only the national and local news and tell me how this affects your worldview. Better yet, watch CNN or FOXNews for twenty-four hours straight. You'll likely think this whole world and everyone in it is evil incarnate. If you focus on what is lacking in your life or relationship, you'll become consumed with how to "fix it." Which often means you'll work harder to get your spouse to change rather than yourself.

Instead, begin practicing contentment in your own life and see what happens.

Notice, it's *practicing* contentment, which is different from being content.

To practice contentment is to engage in an ongoing and conscious process of being aware of your own contentment. It is to continually remind yourself of what there is in your life to be grateful for. It is to become more and more aware that today you already have everything you really need.

What would it take for you, right now, to practice contentment?

It can be as simple as saying this: For me, for now, this is enough. I am content.

Here are six keys to practicing contentment in your life:

**1. Be grateful.** You cannot have contentment without gratitude—the two are inseparable. A grateful person is one who can shift their focus to the good things in their life. When you notice that you're focusing on the things you lack, make a list of the things you're grateful for. A list of all the good things in your life. Write them down. You'll discover that you have a great deal to be grateful for and the feelings of deficiency will diminish.

**2. Take control of your attitude.** It is easy to fall into "when and then thinking": "When I get _______, then I will be happy." Instead, choose your outlook and attitude. Take control of your life. Happiness is fleeting, and it is also not found in the acquisition of possessions. Happiness is based solely on your decision to be happy—and this may be one of the most important life lessons you'll ever learn.

**3. Break the habit of satisfying discontentment with possessions.** It has been ingrained into society that the proper way to defuse discontentment is to purchase the "thing" that is seemingly causing the discontentment. Little energy is spent determining the true root of the discontentment. Are you dissatisfied with your wardrobe? Go buy new clothes. Not content with your vehicle? Get a new one.

We have gotten into the habit of satisfying discontent by spending more money. Material possessions will never fully satisfy the desires of your heart (that's why discontentment always returns and happiness is so fleeting). The next time you recognize discontentment in your life, refuse to give into the desire to spend. Instead, commit to better understanding yourself and why the lack material possessions is causing discontentment. Only after you intentionally break this habit will true contentment begin to surface.

**4. Stop comparing yourself to others.** Comparing your life with someone else's always leads to discontentment. There will always be people who "appear" to be better off than you and seemingly living the perfect life. But be advised, we always compare the worst of what we know about ourselves to the best assumptions that we make about others. Their life is never as perfect as your mind makes it out to be. Know this paraphrase from Proverbs: No one is great to those with whom they live.

**5. Help others.** When you help others, sharing your talents, time, or money, you'll learn to be content. This practice will give you a finer appreciation for what you own, who you are, and what you have to offer.

**6. Be content with what you have, never with what you are.** Never stop learning, growing, or discovering. Take pride in yourself and the progress you have made in life. Also, never forget that life is a journey, not a destination. You can always find room for improvement and growth. Contentment is not the same as complacency. As soon as you stop growing, you start dying.

*Whatever the tasks, do them slowly with ease, in mindfulness, do not do any tasks with the goal of getting them over with. Resolve to each job in a relaxed way, with all your attention. - Thich Nhat Hanh*

*Adapted from Joshua Becker of http://www.becomingminimalist.com

# Simple Rest

In academia, professors have the option of taking a sabbatical for the purpose of expanding their intellectual horizons. They might spend this time doing research in the field, teaching at another university, or writing a book. For those who work in a world without tenure and tweed jackets with patches on the elbows, taking a step back from professional life and finding a little perspective isn't as easy. *But it's still necessary.*

Luckily, I've found that the quality of a sabbatical leave can compensate for a lack of quantity.

Enter . . . the twenty-four-hour sabbatical.

Why take a sabbatical?

At points in our professional and personal lives, we are swept up in the flow of events. As milestones and markers fly past, we promise ourselves that we'll take a deep breath and look around as soon as things slow down. But they don't. When one project is finally wrapping up, three more kick into gear.

Forget smelling the roses, we forget to taste our morning coffee.

To be clear, a one-day sabbatical is *not* a weekly review. It is not an opportunity to catch up on less urgent tasks, reprioritize our to-do lists, or brainstorm on projects. **It is an opportunity you grant yourself to get a little perspective.**

A one-day sabbatical will:

- Recharge your emotional and intellectual batteries
- Stimulate your creativity
- Suggest new directions for your efforts
- Highlight areas in your life that aren't worth the effort
- Awaken long-buried emotions and memories

What do you do when you hang a picture on the wall? If you're like me, you walk a few feet away, then turn quickly and look to see if it's really crooked or not. That's what a sabbatical is all about: getting far enough away to see the big picture.

**How to Take Your Sabbatical**

Your first question might be, why twenty-four hours? In reality, you'll only be gone for eight or ten hours. But the first step is to get terrific sleep beforehand.

Get up bright and early the day before your sabbatical, which, unless you're a freelancer who can make your own schedule, will likely be a Saturday or Sunday. Then get to bed as early as you can manage. Set your alarm to wake up before dawn, before your spouse and kids, and get on the road.

### Pack Your Sabbatical Kit

Prepare a small bag. You'll be on your feet a lot so you want to travel light. Bring:

- ❖ A paperback book
- ❖ A journal and/or voice recorder
- ❖ Pens
- ❖ Bottled water
- ❖ Snack bars, fruit
- ❖ iPod (no podcasts)

Do not bring work. Do not bring a laptop. No iPhone, no Blackberry, no cell phone whatsoever.

Wear comfortable clothes and your best walking shoes or sneakers.

**Choose Your Path**

If you live in a big city, embarking on your sabbatical may be as simple as picking a direction and walking. The main thing is to walk somewhere off your own beaten path. If you're in a suburban area, drive somewhere long unvisited.

Useful sabbatical activities include:

- Perusing a major library
- Visiting a local art or natural history museum
- Strolling along the nearest lake or, if available, seaside
- Eating unfamiliar foods

The point is to allow yourself to spend one full day separated from the tasks and obligations of your life—which is not to say, don't think about your job or your family.

Once you step back from the immediate, practical concerns, you may start thinking about your job or life as a whole. Maybe it's time to accept that your career doesn't make you happy and never will. Or, it may occur to you how lucky you are to be in your position.

In the first case, you might start brainstorming ideas for a career transition. In the latter, you might decide to come back on Monday morning with renewed vigor and dedication.

**The Return**

Spend the day out of the house, away from work, without your gadgets, and I guarantee you'll return at the end of the day feeling, on some level, transformed. Your journal will be full of new ideas. You'll be physically tired but mentally recharged.

Don't worry about processing all those notes right now. A few will be gems; most will seem like they were written by a drunk person in the light of day. Get another good night's sleep, which is an essential step in absorbing any new experience, and take a look in the morning.

There, you've taken a sabbatical, just like an academic. Now, off you go to find a tweed jacket with patches.

*Taken from http://www.lifeclever.com

# Simplicity with kids

If you're a parent, you know that kids create clutter like nobody's business.

It's enough to drive many people crazy, especially people like me who try to keep things as simple as possible. Still, with a little diligence, and a little bit of self-soothing, **it's possible to have a simple, (relatively) uncluttered home as well as peace of mind.**

Let me first state the obvious: Any life that includes children is going to be complicated, at least to some degree. You'll never get an absolute minimalist lifestyle with kids.

**However, I have found ways to simplify my house, including the kids' rooms**. Sure, the house still gets messy. But it's not as bad as it once was, and it's at a manageable level.

Here are some tips for simplifying your home with kids (adapted from my friend Leo of Zen Habits):

**1. Identify the important.** The first step in decluttering is identifying which toys and other possessions are truly important to the kids. What do they play with, what do they love? Then get rid of as much of the rest as possible, keeping only those things they use and love.

**2. Massively purge.** In the beginning, if you have a lot of kid clutter, you'll want to do a massive purge. Block off a day to go through their rooms. Do one area at a time: a drawer, a section of the closet, a shelf. Take everything out of that area and put it in a pile. From that pile, take only the really important stuff (see tip 1). Get rid of the rest. Donate it to charity if it's still good. Get some boxes for the donations, and when the boxes are full, load them in your car to donate on your next trip. Then put back the keepers, and tackle the next area. If you do this quickly, you can do a room in a couple of hours.

**3. Leave space.** When you put the important stuff back, don't try to fill up each drawer, shelf, or closet area. Allow some space around the objects. It's much nicer looking, and it leaves room for a couple of extra items later if necessary.

**4. Contain.** The key for us has been to contain the kid clutter. Our kids keep their stuff in their rooms. The living room, kitchen, and dining room are for household stuff only, except during play times when there are trains and cars and stuffed animals everywhere (see tip 11). At the end of the day, however, we try to get everything back where it belongs.

**5. Bins.** Bins or baskets are the best containers for kids' stuff. The key is to make it easy for the kids (or you) to toss their stuff into the bins, making cleanup simple. Label each bin (blocks, stuffed animals, Legos). If your child can't read, use pictures.

**6. Cubbies.** Cubbies are great for little toys. They don't take up much room in closets or on a shelf, and they give kids a place to put their little odds and ends.

**7. A home for everything.** We haven't completely succeeded at this, but we try to teach the kids that everything they own has a "home." This means that if they're going to put away a toy, they should know where its home is, and put it there. If they don't know where the home is, they need to find a home for it, and put it there from now on. Actually, this is a useful concept for adults, too.

**8. Organize like with like.** Keep similar things organized together—one bin for stuffed animals, another for sports stuff, another for cars. This makes it easier to remember where things go. Same thing with clothes: underwear and socks together, shirts, shorts, pants, etc.

**9. One place for school papers.** Similarly, you should have one place to keep all incoming school papers. And when you get a school calendar or notification of a school event, enter it in a Google calendar or write it on a calendar in the kitchen

**10. Teach your kids to clean**. Obviously a one-year-old won't know how to clean up after themselves, but older kids do. So, instead of continually stressing out about the messes, just ask them to clean up now and then. Sure, things will get messy again soon. But at least the kids are doing the work cleaning up, not you.

**11. Allow them to make a mess.** Kids are not perfect. They will inevitably make a mess. You have to allow them to do this. Then, when they're done, ask them to clean it up. No harm, no foul.

**12. Purge at Christmas and birthdays.** On these two occasions, new stuff comes into our kids' lives en masse. If you just add the new stuff to the old stuff, you will have a huge mess. Instead, ask them to put all their gifts in one place. Then, a day or two after Christmas or their birthday, go through their closets and bins and ask them what they want to get rid of so they can make room for the new stuff.

**13. Do regular decluttering.** Every month or two, you'll need to declutter their stuff. (see tip 1). Do this at least quarterly. You could put a reminder in your calendar, or just look at their room every now and then, and if it looks way too cluttered, schedule some time to purge.

**14. Less is more**. Teach your kids that they don't need tons of stuff to be happy. They can't possibly play with everything anyway—there aren't enough hours in a day. With less stuff, they can find things more easily, they can see what there is to play with, and they can own better quality stuff (see next tip).

**15. Go for quality.** Instead of getting your kids a huge pile of cheap junk, go for quality toys or possessions that will last a long time. Wood is better than plastic, for example. The classic toys are often the best. One of my son's favorite toys is my old Tonka truck—you remember those, the kind that were metal and big and could really hurt someone if thrown. It's best to spend your money on a couple of great things than a whole bunch of cheap stuff that will break and be relegated to the junk pile in no time.

**16. Learn to accept.** You'll never have a minimal life with kids. You have to accept this.

**17. Buy less.** Drastically reduce the amount of stuff you buy for your kids. It's difficult to resist them when they really want something at a store, I know, but you aren't doing them any favors by caving in. Don't deprive them completely, but also don't spoil them with stuff. On Christmas, for example, just get them a few great things rather than a whole bunch of stuff.

**18. Clean as you go.** I've learned to clean up messes as I go (or ask the kids to clean up theirs) so the house isn't a wreck. This is especially helpful when the kids transition from one plaything to another. Simply have them pick up one before they get the next one out.

**19. Clean before bed.** I also do a quick cleanup right before I go to bed, getting anything the little ones forgot to put away. It makes mornings much more pleasant.

**20. Thirty-minute cleanups**. On Saturdays, try a "thirty-minute cleanup." This means that every child (over the age of four or five probably) has a chore, and the whole family (including parents) pitches in to clean. Set a timer and see if you can do it all in thirty minutes. This teaches kids that there are responsibilities that come along with things (and being part of a family). It also gives you a clean house and the rest of the day to have fun.

**21. Prep time.** This isn't so much to do with clutter as with general simplifying your life with kids. It helps to have prep time each evening and morning to prepare the kids' lunches, clothes, or whatever is needed for the day. This means we get the soccer gear and drinks and snacks ready on soccer days, or whatever gear is necessary for that day. It saves a rush when you are trying to get out the door, and saves you from forgetting stuff later.

*Adapted from Leo Babauta of http://zenhabits.net

# Simplicity with family

If there is one thing that will throw a wrench in married life, it's kids.

Don't get me wrong, kids are a tremendous blessing and a source of fun and laughter, but they can also be whiny, energy-draining monsters who can suck joy out of life at the drop of a hat.

With kids around the house, no matter what their ages, life gets more complicated and busy with activities, homework, chores, meals, bedtimes, carpools, and on it goes.

Much of how we "do" family is learned and passed down through the generations. Each generation either adopts what their family did, or goes to the extreme, vowing to do family vastly different from the previous generation.

Either way, your past influences your present.

And your present will influence your kids' futures.

How great would it be to pass along a simple, loving, passionate, adventurous marriage to your future generations?

It can be done, and it's easier than you think.

It begins by slowing down and making a note of all you do in your marriage during a typical week. Seriously, take a moment and write it all down. Not things you do for your children, not things you do for your job or career, not the things you do so the house looks the way you'd like, but the things you do with your spouse.

If you're like most people, this little exercise will be a bit disheartening. You'll likely see that your marriage is often pushed aside for other things.

It is so easy to replace the important with the immediate.

Research is now revealing that when priority is placed on the marriage and not the children, the children, and, not surprisingly, the marriage, both benefit.

On a side note: Care to guess the second highest time-frame for divorce? Twenty-plus years of marriage. The reason? Kids are gone and there's little to hold the couple together.

So regardless where you find yourself currently, if you work on making your marriage a priority, your kids reap the benefits.

So do you.

Here are a few ideas that may help:

**1. Steal moments together.** If you have young children in the house like I do, it's difficult to find times to connect with your spouse. Take advantage of bedtime routines. My wife and I have short discussions while the kids are in the bathtub. We sit together on the deck after they go to bed. Look for moments throughout your day, and you'll likely find many opportunities.

**2. Make it clear that you love your spouse.** It's been stated that one of the best things you can do for your children is love their mom/dad. This is true, but it goes beyond just saying it. Sit together while watching a movie or TV. Hug. Kiss. Talk. Cuddle. All in front of your kids.

**3. Do things as a family, but for your marriage.** Go on walks. Ride bikes. Eat outside. Play. Go on vacation. Go to the playground and not only push your kids in the swing, push your spouse as well. It's the little things you do together that will create lasting bonds for your marriage *and* your family.

**4. Go on dates.** Take advantage of family members who live nearby or contribute to the economy of a local teenager by hiring them to babysit so you and your spouse can go out for an evening. It may take some planning, but it's worth it. Make a point to have an evening alone with your spouse at least once a month. And change up what you do on dates. Go on an adventure, eat at a new restaurant, try something different. The point is, add a bit of novelty to your relationship and your dates. It will create a spark between you.

**5. Give up the TV.** We go without the TV for the month of August and it's amazing to see what this does for our marriage. Try it for a week, or limit the shows you watch and use that time to talk, do little projects together, or spend the time in other pursuits (wink, wink).

**6. Declutter.** Clutter distracts, adds chaos, and drains energy from life and relationships. Give your marriage a boost by decluttering the master bedroom. Nothing can kill a romantic moment like embracing your lover, kissing passionately, making your way to the bed together only to trip over the pile of clothes on the floor. Spend some time this weekend decluttering your room. The rest of the house can wait.

# Simple Money

My wife is a CPA—and at the risk of offending the CPA society, your brains are just wired differently than the rest of ours. That is definitely the case with my wife.

I consider myself to be fairly good with numbers, and I did well in math, but I'm not in the league of the CPA—although I do find great pleasure when my checkbook balances and hers is off a few cents. She returns the joy by poking fun at how long it takes me to complete the one-star Sudoku puzzle.

From the beginning of our marriage, she preferred to live within a budget. At first I would enter the discussions kicking and screaming. I always felt a budget was far too limiting. I didn't want to cramp my style.

Needless to say, my attitude helped get us in a financial hole.

When it comes to a budget, there are those who live by one and those who swear tomorrow they are going to sit down and write one out. The intention is honest, they just have trouble following through.

So how do you set up a budget you'll actually follow?

Glad you asked. To begin, remember this one simple rule: **Spend less money than you make.**

Now that we covered the main idea, let's create a simple budget that even the greatest procrastinators can follow (if they ever get around to it).

**Step 1: Have a conversation with your cash.**

We place meaning on things. Money is no different. What does your money mean to you? What value does it provide? Beyond providing basic necessities like food, shelter, and keeping Mr. Tax Man from visiting, what's your money for? Security. Fun. Power. Fame. Understanding the meaning you place on money can go a long way in helping you get your money under control.

**Step 2: Where does your money go?**

Every budget begins with an understanding of where your money goes on a day-to-day basis. Don't skip this step. If you don't know where it all goes, you won't be able to determine where you want it to go.

There are two ways to go about this: the CPA way, tracking your spending for at least three months, inputting every penny in a multi-category, macro-enabled Excel spreadsheet, and pouring over every debit and credit each night; or the lazy person's way.

Lazy it is! For those who use credit or debit cards for most of their spending (paid off in full each month, of course), review the monthly statements and categorize your spending areas. Some cards do this already.

If you live on cold, hard cash, write down all your expenditures for one week, then multiply the numbers by four (there's that pesky math again) to get a rough idea of where your cash goes. This method obviously is leaving out the major monthly expenses like house, car, insurance, and the like. Simply add these numbers to the monthly estimate. Simple, eh?

If you chose the CPA way, at this point you would add up each column of the spreadsheet, run the macro/algorithm you've created in your spare time on Friday night, and analyze the results by running the final numbers through the statistical program you're bound to have on your laptop.

**Step 3: Plan how to spend your cash.**

Now that you know where your money goes, it's time to spend your hard-earned cash. Not literally yet. Sorry. Instead, make a list of expenses for the upcoming three to six months, including vacations, car tune-ups, paying off debt, saving, or investing in your favorite mutual fund. Do the same for long-term plans, two to five years out.

You now have a spending plan. Be sure to leave a little room for the unexpected cash you're sure to need at times, like when your car breaks down or your in-laws decide to move in for a few months.

**Step 4: That pesky math again.**

With your spending plan in front of you, add in items from your "wish list," then calculate what these items would run you on a monthly basis. For instance, for the upcoming family vacation, divide the total cost by the number of months until the trip. Voilà, you have a way to prepare for the trip and pay for it as you go.

**Step 5: Save money the no-brainer way.**

This is really simple. Visit your bank and set up an automatic monthly transfer from your checking account to savings. This could be as little as $20 a month. No worries.

**This is important: Put something into savings every month.**

**Step 6: Cut out the frivolous spending.**

The list of "must-have" items is endless. To curb the frivolous purchase's impact on your overall spending plans, try the "envelope" system. It's easy:

- ❖ Come up with a reasonable weekly amount to spend in your biggest categories: food (or, depending on your lifestyle, get more specific such as "lunch," "family dinners out"); entertainment (e.g., happy hours, movies, tabloids); transportation (gas, parking, taxis, public transportation); apparel/services (dry cleaning, haircuts, cute shoes.)

  For guidance, consider that the four big-budget categories in a typical American household are housing (34%), transportation (18%), food (13%), and entertainment (4%).

- ❖ Create envelopes for each of those categories.

- ❖ Put the allotted amount of cash to cover a week's or month's worth of expenses into each envelope. (You don't have to carry the entire wad with you every day, but do make sure you don't cheat with extra visits to the ATM.)

- ❖ Once the cash is gone, so is your weekly stipend.

Remember, once you get a handle on your finances, you'll free up more time to worry and fight about other things. But look at it this way: you'll have more money to go out on a nice date when you make up.

*Adapted from The Motley Fool, http://www.fool.com

Made in the USA
Middletown, DE
18 September 2017